by Kevin Blake

Consultant: Marjorie Faulstich Orellana, PhD
Professor of Urban Schooling
University of California, Los Angeles

New York, New York

Credits

Cover, © iagodina/iStock and © Beriliu/Dreamstime; TOC, © Le Do/Shutterstock; 4, © RossHelen/Shutterstock; 5T, © LianeM/Shutterstock; 5B, © fotoNino/Shutterstock; 7, © Sun_Shine/Shutterstock; 8T, © istankov/iStock; 8B, © Jovan Vidakovic/Shutterstock; 9, © DuxX/Shutterstock; 10L, © David Havel/Shutterstock; 10–11, © Drazen Boskic PHOTO/Shutterstock; 11R, © Freder/iStock; 12T, © Alexey Stiop/Shutterstock; 12B, © Nataliia Bornia/Dreamstime; 13, © Roberto Nistri/Alamy; 14, © Caro/Andree Kaiser/Newscom; 15T, © Paolo Siccardi/Marka/AGE Fotostock; 15B, © Northfoto/Shutterstock; 16, © dinosmichail/Shutterstock; 17, © Dado Ruvic/Reuters/Newscom; 18–19, © Xantana/iStock; 19R, © Henrique Weiss/Dreamstime; 20, © sduraku/Shutterstock; 21, © underworld/Shutterstock; 22–23, © Nina Jovic/Shutterstock; 23R, © sumbul/iStock; 24L, © Xinhua/Alamy; 24–25, © Mgntplus/Dreamstime; 26, © BasicPhoto/Shutterstock; 27, © Adel Basic/Dreamstime; 28, © Fotokon/Dreamstime; 29, © Veronika Kovalenko/Shutterstock; 30T, © Andrej Safaric/Shutterstock, © SabinaS/iStock, and © Vitoria Holdings LLC/iStock; 30B, © Associated Press/AP Images; 31 (T to B), © Impact Photography/Shutterstock, © fotokon/iStock, © kriphoto/Shutterstock, © vpopovic/iStock, and © Rudmer Zwerver/Shutterstock; 32, © rook76/Shutterstock.

Publisher: Kenn Goin
Senior Editor: Joyce Tavolacci
Creative Director: Spencer Brinker
Design: Debrah Kaiser
Photo Researcher: Thomas Persano

Library of Congress Cataloging-in-Publication Data

Names: Blake, Kevin, 1978– author.
Title: Bosnia and Herzegovina / by Kevin Blake.
Description: New York, New York : Bearport Publishing, [2020] | Series:
  Countries we come from | Includes bibliographical references and index.
Identifiers: LCCN 2019007160 (print) | LCCN 2019010929 (ebook) | ISBN
  9781642805758 (ebook) | ISBN 9781642805215 (library bound)
Subjects: LCSH: Bosnia and Herzegovina—Juvenile literature.
Classification: LCC DR1660 (ebook) | LCC DR1660 .B55 2020 (print) | DDC
  949.742—dc23
LC record available at https://lccn.loc.gov/2019007160

For more information, write to Bearport Publishing Company, Inc., 45 West 21st Street, Suite 3B, New York, New York 10010. Printed in the United States of America.

10 9 8 7 6 5 4 3 2 1

Contents

This Is Bosnia and Herzegovina

Beautiful

HISTORIC

Interesting

Welcome to Bosnia (BOZ-nee-uh) and Herzegovina (her-tsuh-goh-VEE-nuh)!

This small country is in Europe.

It includes two regions—Bosnia and Herzegovina.

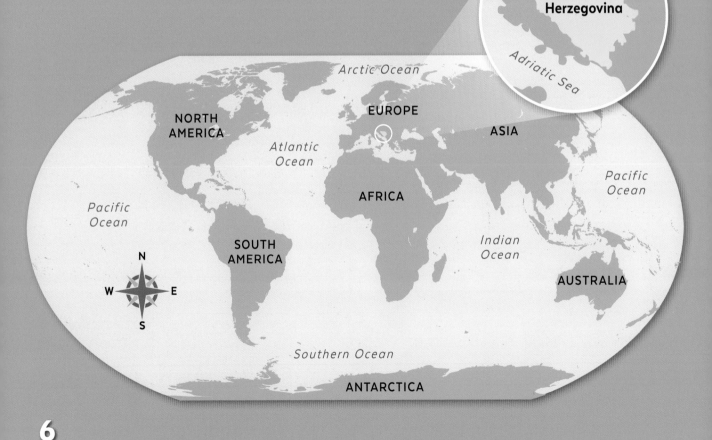

EUROPE

Bosnia and Herzegovina

Adriatic Sea

Arctic Ocean

NORTH AMERICA

EUROPE

ASIA

Atlantic Ocean

Pacific Ocean

AFRICA

Pacific Ocean

Indian Ocean

SOUTH AMERICA

AUSTRALIA

N
W E
S

Southern Ocean

ANTARCTICA

Almost four million people live in Bosnia and Herzegovina. The country is often simply called Bosnia.

Bosnia has many **majestic** mountains.

The tallest one is called Maglić (maj-LEEK).

It's 7,828 feet (2,386 m) high!

Maglić is part of a mountain range called the Alps.

Leafy forests cover much of the country.

Beautiful animals live in Bosnia.

Wild horses roam the mountains.

Red foxes pounce on **prey**.

Some of the largest animals in Bosnia are brown bears.

Bosnia is home to different groups of people.

The three main groups are the Bosniaks (boz-NEE-aks), Serbs, and Croats (KROW-atz).

Each group has its own language and **culture**.

Most Bosnians are either Muslim or Christian.

Bosnia used to be part of a country called Yugoslavia.

In 1992, many Bosniaks and Croats voted for Bosnia to be its own nation.

Yet a lot of Serbs wanted to remain a part of Yugoslavia.

This started a horrible war.

Yugoslavia split into six different countries in 1992.

The war lasted for over three long years.

In 1995, the groups stopped fighting.

To keep the peace, Bosnia now has three presidents—one from each group.

Bosnia's three presidents

Over 100,000 people died in the war.

The **capital** of Bosnia is Sarajevo (sar-uh-YEY-voh).

It's also the country's largest city.

More than 275,000 people live there.

people playing chess

Banja Luka (BAHN-yah LOO-kah) is the second-largest city in Bosnia.

Bosnia has three main languages: Bosnian, Croatian, and Serbian.

This is how you say *mountain* in all three languages:

Planina (plah-NEE-nah)

Serbian uses its own alphabet.

This is how *mountain* is written in Serbian:

планина

a sign in Bosnian and Serbian

Bosna i Hercegovina
Босна и Херцеговина

Many people in Bosnia also speak English.

Bosnian food is full of flavor!

Meals often include vegetables, cream called *pavlaka*, and meat.

Cevapi is grilled meat and bread.

For dessert, people enjoy baklava. It's a sweet pastry filled with nuts and honey.

What sports do people play in Bosnia?

Bosnians enjoy soccer. Children start playing when they're very young.

Basketball is another popular sport in Bosnia.

Bosnians love folk music.

People often play violins and accordions.

accordion

Sevdah is a type of Bosnian folk music.

Dancers move to the lively music!

Drinking coffee is a popular pastime.

People sit for hours in **cafés**.

The coffee is served in a metal pot with a long neck.

It's thick and rich. *Yum!*

Bosnian coffee has a strong chocolaty flavor.

Fast Facts

Capital city: Sarajevo

Population of Bosnia and Herzegovina: About four million

Main languages: Bosnian, Croatian, and Serbian

Money: Bosnian mark

Major religions: Islam, Russian Orthodox, and Roman Catholic

Neighboring countries: Croatia, Montenegro, and Serbia

Cool Fact: Sarajevo was the location of the 1984 Winter Olympics!

cafés (KA-feyz) places where people meet for coffee and light food

capital (KAP-uh-tuhl) the city where a country's government is based

culture (KUL-tuhr) the ideas, customs, and traditions shared by a group of people

majestic (mah-JES-tik) having impressive beauty

prey (PRAY) an animal that is hunted and eaten by another animal

31

Index

Read More

Filipović, Zlata. *Zlata's Diary: A Child's Life in Wartime Sarajevo.* New York: Penguin (2006).

Mulla-Feroze, Umaima. *Welcome to Bosnia and Herzegovina (Welcome to My Country).* Milwaukee, WI: Gareth Stevens (2001).

Learn More Online

To learn more about Bosnia and Herzegovina, visit
www.bearportpublishing.com/CountriesWeComeFrom

About the Author

Kevin Blake lives in Providence, Rhode Island, with his wife, Melissa, his son, Sam, and his daughter, Ilana. He'd love to take a trip to Bosnia soon!